DISCOVER
GREAT WHITE SHARKS

by Virginia Loh-Hagan

Cherry Lake Publishing • Ann Arbor, Michigan

3

Published in the United States of America
by Cherry Lake Publishing
Ann Arbor, Michigan
www.cherrylakepublishing.com

Content Adviser: Dr. Jelle Atema, Professor of Marine Biology at Boston
University and adjunct scientist at the Woods Hole Oceanographic Institution
Reading Adviser: Marla Conn, ReadAbility, Inc

Photo Credits: © Stefan Pircher/Shutterstock Images, cover;
© Creativa Images/Shutterstock Images, 4; © BW Folsom/Shutterstock Images
© Havoc/Shutterstock Images, 8; © Sergey Uryadnikov, 10, 20; © Ethan Daniels
Shutterstock Images, 12; © Elsa Hoffman/Shutterstock Images, 14; mingis/
Shutterstock Images, 16; © holbox/Shutterstock Images, 18

Library of Congress Cataloging-in-Publication Data
Loh-Hagan, Virginia, author.
  Discover great white sharks / by Virginia Loh-Hagan.
    pages cm. —(Splash!)
  Summary: "This Level 3 guided reader introduces basic facts about great
white sharks, including their physical characteristics, diet, and habitat. Simple
callouts ask the student to think in new ways, supporting inquiry-based
reading. Additional text features and search tools, including a glossary and a
index, help students locate information and learn new words."— Provided by
publisher.
  Audience: Ages 6–10
  Audience: K to grade 3
  Includes bibliographical references and index.
  ISBN 978-1-63362-598-3 (hardcover) — ISBN 978-1-63362-688-1 (pbk.) —
ISBN 978-1-63362-778-9 (pdf) — ISBN 978-1-63362-868-7 (ebook)
  1. White shark—Juvenile literature. I. Title.

QL638.95.L3L64 2016
597.3'3—dc23
                                                    2014050236

Cherry Lake Publishing would like to acknowledge the work of the Partnership
for 21st Century Skills. Please visit www.p21.org for more information.

Printed in the United States of America
Corporate Graphics

TABLE OF CONTENTS

Giant Predators

Great white sharks are the largest **predatory** fish. They can grow to be 20 feet (6 meters) long. They can weigh 4,000 pounds (1,814 kilograms).

A great white shark is one of the heaviest fish in the ocean.

Great whites have five rows of sharp teeth. Their teeth get stuck in whatever they bite! They lose and replace teeth all the time.

Science museums often put great white shark teeth on display.

Great white sharks use **gills** to breathe. Tooth-like scales, or **denticles**, cover their skin. They don't have bones. They have **cartilage**.

Great white sharks breathe with their gills.

Talented Hunters

Great white sharks are named for their white bellies. But they are dark on top. This helps them **ambush** their **prey**. The prey can't see them swimming through the water.

THINK! Great white sharks hardly ever become prey. The only animals that will attack them are orca whales and other great white sharks. What would happen if the ocean had too many great white sharks in one area? Or what if too many of them were killed?

This great white shark is preying on a seal.

Great white sharks have special organs. They can hear, smell, and see very well. They roll their eyes back in their heads when they attack. This protects their eyes.

Great white sharks hunt with their strong senses.

Tiny holes dot the area around a shark's **snout**. These holes sense the **electricity** given off by other moving animals.

Great white sharks also have special organs on the sides of their bodies. These organs help them sense the direction their prey is moving.

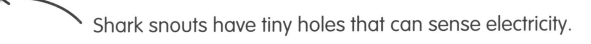

Shark snouts have tiny holes that can sense electricity.

SHARK
SIGHTED
TODAY

ENTER WATER
AT OWN
RISK

Ocean Protectors

Falling coconuts kill more people than great white sharks. They don't want to eat humans. We taste bad to them! But a great white shark might attack a swimmer or surfer if it thinks he or she is a seal.

LOOK!

Read this sign. What would you add to it or take off of it? Why is it important for swimmers to know that sharks are nearby?

Some beaches post shark warning signs.

Great white sharks eat injured and sick animals. They also eat whale **carcasses**.

Great white sharks are **solitary** animals. They usually hunt alone. But sometimes, they work together to move whale carcasses that they can share.

Sharks sometimes eat dead whales, like this one.

We need great white sharks. There are only 10,000 of them left in the world. Without them, there would be too many animals. They keep the oceans **balanced**.

CREATE!

Create a list describing how great white sharks are like fish. Also, describe how they differ. For example: Like fish, great white sharks are hatched from eggs. Unlike most fish, shark eggs stay inside their mothers until they are born.

The ocean needs great white sharks.

Think About It

Great white sharks lived before the dinosaurs. Why have they been able to survive longer than most animals? Why haven't they changed much in millions of years?

Great white sharks are one of only a couple kinds of sharks known to attack humans. But crocodiles, pigs, elephants, and dogs kill more people than great white sharks. Why do you think great white sharks have such a bad reputation? (Some people refer to these sharks as "White Death.")

Find Out More

BOOK

Westwood, Brett. *Great White Shark: Habitats, Life Cycles, Food Chains, Threats*. Austin, TX: Raintree Steck-Vaughn, 2000.

WEB SITE
Smithsonian National Museum of Natural History Ocean Portal—Great White Shark
http://ocean.si.edu/great-white-shark
Read some basic facts about great white sharks.

Glossary

ambush (AM-bush) to attack from a hiding place

balanced (BAL-uhnsd) having an even number of something, such as predators and prey

carcasses (KAR-kuhs-iz) dead bodies of animals

cartilage (KAHR-tuh-lij) flexible and bendable material or tissue; your nose and ears are made of cartilage

denticles (DEN-tih-kuhlz) tiny, hard flakes that cover and protect the skin of sharks

electricity (ih-lek-TRIS-i-tee) a form of energy; in the ocean, electricity is created by animals when they move

gill slits (GIL slitz) openings that let water flow out of the gills, which are organs to let the fish breathe underwater; water flows in through the mouth

predatory (PRED-uh-tor-ee) living by eating other animals

prey (PRAY) animals that are eaten by other animals

snout (SNOUT) the tip of the shark that includes the nose and mouth

solitary (SAH-li-ter-ee) not requiring the companionship of others

Index

About the Author

Dr. Virginia Loh-Hagan is an author, university professor, former classroom teacher, and curriculum designer. Ever since seeing *Jaws*, she's been scared of great white sharks—until she wrote this book and learned more about them! She lives in San Diego with her very tall husband and very naughty dogs. To learn more about her, visit www.virginialoh.com.